Short Voyages

Edited by Chris Buckton and Pie Corbett

Contents

OXFORD
UNIVERSITY PRESS

THE GREY GANDER

A story set in Tudor times

Wat's fingers were so cold they seemed made of wood. His feet were wet through. He shivered as he drove the geese towards the pen. He could hardly see the gate for the rain blowing in his eyes.

The geese went into the pen easily enough. But the bad-tempered old gander stuck its neck out, long and low, and charged, with its wings spread wide. Wat cursed and poked it with his stick. He hated the old gander. Bringing the geese home was the worst job in the day.

All the children had jobs to do. The oldest boys worked for the Lord of the manor with their father. They looked after the Lord's sheep. The oldest girls helped their mother to make medicines out of the plants they gathered. Wat, who was the youngest, had to do the jobs that nobody else wanted to do, like emptying the privy or fetching wood. And taking the three geese to graze on the village green and bringing them back at the end of the day.

The gander hissed and pecked Wat's fingers as he slammed the gate. He didn't check the latch. He was in too much of a hurry to get out of the rain.

Inside the cottage it was smoky and warm. His mother put a steaming pot on the table. "The bacon's all gone," she said. "We must make do with turnips."

"Never fret," said Wat's father. "We will eat a goose soon for Christmas dinner. Good meat, as well as a bowl full of fat, to rub on our chests against the cold."

"Let's eat the old gander!" said Wat.

Wat's father shook his head. "No. He's our watchman. His honking keeps the fox away."

Something woke Wat that night. A honking. He remembered what his father had said. The gander was keeping the fox away. He pulled the covers round him, snuggled up against his brother's warm back, and fell asleep again.

But in the morning there was a terrible sight. The gate swung loose, and there were feathers and blood in the mud. The two geese were huddled together at the end of the pen. The gander had gone.

Wat noticed a trail through the mud towards the wood behind their cottage. The fox must have dragged the gander that way. If he could find it, they could still eat it for Christmas.

The trail ended by an old tree. He could see the foxes' den under its roots. There were more feathers and blood, but no gander.

Wat picked up a handful of feathers and let them fall like snowflakes. He knew how the fox had got in. He hadn't fastened the gate. He would get a thrashing. And there would be no Christmas dinner. The family couldn't afford to lose a gander as well as a goose.

He picked up some grey wing feathers and stuck them in his belt. At least he could use them to tip his arrows. As he stood up he caught sight of a dark shape amongst the bushes. He moved cautiously towards it, his stick raised. A wolf maybe, or a neighbour's dog?

It was a young ram, struggling to free itself from a tangle of bushes. Wat climbed on to its broad back, holding tight to its fleece, pressing his legs to its sides to keep its body still. Then he pushed its head down with one hand, and tore at the branches with the other.

It was free! Wat looped his cloak round the ram's neck, and led it back through the rain.

"It's the Lord's ram!" exclaimed his father, when Wat told him what had happened. He seemed more worried about that than the lost gander.

"We must get it to the fold. I must have failed to fasten the gate. If the Lord finds that it's missing…" His voice trailed away, and his hand trembled as he took the ram from Wat. Wat knew that if they displeased their Lord, they would lose everything. Their work, their cottage, everything.

But it was too late. When they reached the fold, the Lord was standing by the gate. "What now, Goodman Green? Where are you taking my best ram?"

Wat's father tugged his son's sleeve, and together they bowed low. Wat peeped sideways to look at the Lord's face. He couldn't tell if he was angry or jesting.

"And what are these?" The Lord tweaked at the feathers stuck in Wat's belt.

Wat started to explain. The words tumbled out, and tears too.

The Lord's frown changed into laughter.

"No Christmas dinner? What do you say, Goodman Green? "

Wat's father hung his head, not sure what to say. The Lord gave a great bellow of laughter. It made Wat jump.

"Two gates left open, father and son! But a quick wit has won the day. And your reward shall be –" The Lord slapped Wat heartily on the back.

"– a goose for Christmas!"

Wat and his father shared a silent, nervous smile.

Chris Buckton

Wave-Eater

Viking legend tells how Ingolf Arnarson became the first man to settle on Iceland – a warmer, fertile, uninhabited place in those days. Viking families – parents, grandparents, children, cousins, slaves – lived together in longhouses, the huge doorposts elaborately carved with mythical stories. When Ingolf fled Norway, he took his doorposts, stories and family with him. This story springs from the legend that the doorposts reached land before him!

Cold! It bites like a wolf. It grips my ribs so hard I can't get my breath. My icy face can't feel if it's above water or below. I never thought – plgch! – that I'd die so far from home!

We set sail for the north a month ago, looking for somewhere new, somewhere safe from the tyrant who's clutching all Norway in his fists. The ship wallowed under the weight of our animals and baggage. My uncle Floki can usually read the stars as if they are magic maps carved in the sky, but some nights we could not even see the stars!

7

Floki said the northern summer nights are too light for them to show. But I said the wind had blown them all out, or the waves had washed them out of the sky! I had never seen such monstrous waves – not close up. Coward that I am: some days I couldn't swallow my bread for fear.

Floki sent my little brother up the mast, as a look-out. I don't know how he hung on. Wave-Eater would plunge down into a pit of dark, then pitch upwards again. The animals were on their knees, sliding about, boneless with sea-sickness. It took three men on the steering-oar to hold us steady. My mother and aunt climbed into their

bwiseman 04

bedding for warmth. Then everything happened at once.

My brother gave a shout and pointed. "Land! Land?" Floki loosed his ravens – one! – two! – three! – to see if he was right: the birds always fly towards land. Ingolf Arnarson shouted: "Throw my doorposts over the side! Wherever they touch land, there we shall settle!" Two of the men let go the steering–oar to help lift the great slabs of wood. But a huge wave suddenly pulled itself up – high as the masthead – and Wave-Eater hit it sideways. Then all our belongings started to slide…

The plough and a bundle of spears came scraping down the deck – killed a goat and spilled three baskets of grain. They came straight at me! So I jumped – up on to the ship's rail. The rail buckled as we hit another wave. Spray broke over me, then I was in the water and drowning.

I think Father would have jumped in after me, but he was wearing his sword across his back and it would have taken him straight to the bottom. My little brother yelled my name. One of the ravens swooped down as if to peck out my eyes. The boat's wake washed over my head. Wave-Eater sped on and away, and I was alone in the ocean, floundering.

Cold is chewing on me – wolfing me down,
gripping my ribs so tight I can't catch my breath.
Then bang! Something hits my legs under the
water. Too cold to feel the pain, but not the fear.
Is it a whale come to swallow me? It bursts
through the surface, brown and sharp-cornered,
and I see deer – trees – dogs carved into its wood.
It is one of Ingolf Arnarson's doorposts! How
often I have run my fingers over those carvings
while our storytellers told us ancient tales of
voyaging heroes and monsters. I pull myself across
the doorpost, and its partner comes nudging and
prodding alongside.

How long have I clung on? I have no idea. But
the sea around me now has begun to steam – yes,
steam! Land reaches out two arms to me and the
bay between is steaming like soup! The water feels

warm – at least against my purple, dead arms, it feels warm. Shingle rubs my knees and I am ashore. I have landed in a new world, a strange, new world with birch trees … willows!

Now I sit between the two doorposts, facing out to sea. For one small girl, the men of Norway would not come looking. But for these mighty doorposts, relics of our former home, they will come. All I have to do is wait for them. This is where Ingolf has sworn to build our new home. I'll help dig the holes. I'll help replant the doorposts, like twin trees. And we'll put down roots again, in this steamy, starless, new, northern land.

Geraldine McCaughrean

My Name is Jim

A story set in the Second World War

My name is Jim. I want to tell you about the day Ted Baker and I nearly got killed by a German buzz bomb.

These buzz bombs were called doodlebugs. They were like bombs with wings. The Germans sent them up into the air in France and they came down on London. They used to make a really odd *putt putt* noise as they came down. But the worst bit was when they went quiet because then you had 15 seconds before they blew up. Not that I knew any of this on that day. And neither did Ted.

Ted and I were ten. We hated each other. He was a big lad with fat knees and no neck. I was thin in those days. Small. And I had big ears. Ted used to make fun of me. My dad wouldn't fight in the war, you see. He said it was wrong to kill people, and he got sent to jail. That's what happened in those days.

Ted's dad had gone to the war and he was killed. Ted's mum ran the family fruit shop. She mostly sold things like apples and pears and nuts

12

during the war. She had a brother who worked
down at the docks and once, Ted said, he gave her
some bananas. Not to sell – just a few for her and
Ted to eat. I thought Ted was pulling my leg. I
had never seen a banana in my life.

Ted called me Jug-ears. He said my dad was
too scared to go to war and he called him names
too.

We lived in south London and plenty of bombs
fell there; but doodlebugs were a new thing. Lots
of children were sent to live in the country with
strangers so they could be safe. But my mum
wouldn't send me, and neither would Ted's.

I wanted to be sent away. I wanted to get away from Ted. When I went down the road past his mum's shop to school, he would be waiting. He would call me names or take my gas mask. We all had to carry masks, in case the Germans dropped gas bombs on us, but they never did.

Other times he would push me over and rub my face in the dirt. Sometimes I ran away. But he always got me in the end.

Once he grabbed me and shook me until my teeth rattled.

"That's for my dad, you little rat," he shouted. "That's for my dad!" And he kept on until his mum came out of the shop and stopped him. She put her arm round him and took him inside.

Anyway, this morning, I had just turned into the street and I saw Ted. He began to shout the usual old rubbish at me, when we heard this *putt putt* noise. We'd never heard anything like it. *Putt putt, putt putt!* Like a really loud motorbike, and it was coming from the sky.

I shot a quick look at Ted and he was standing there staring up with his mouth wide open.

Other people on the street had stopped too. Nobody knew what this noise was and I can tell you the hair stood up on the back of my neck. And then the air raid sirens started howling and

14

people began to run. When the sirens stopped somebody shouted: "Get to the shelters!" I could see Mrs Smith walking quickly off down the road. It seemed really quiet after the sirens and then I realized I could still hear this *putt putt* noise. Ted was still standing in the road, staring up with his mouth open, just as if he wanted to catch flies. It was like he didn't know what was going on. He looked really stupid.

I don't know why I ran to him, shouting in all that silence. I pushed him off the road just as there was a huge whump! right behind us and we fell sprawling in a heap in his mum's shop doorway with me on top and Ted's face flat on the dusty floor. All sorts of stuff from the blast was falling outside and you could hear glass smashing.

After a while I got up, but Ted still lay there.

"Are you all right?" I asked. He was crying so I patted him on the shoulder. "It's all right," I said. "We're safe." And then Ted's mum came out and we helped him up and looked at the street.

The air was thick with dust. The house at number 42 wasn't there any more. The bomb had landed right inside it. The house next door had just sagged like it was made of wet cardboard. Mrs Smith was lying on the pavement and her hat had fallen off. A load of bricks had fallen on her. There was another load of bricks right where Ted had been standing. He took one look, and was sick.

His mum stared at him and me, and then back at Ted. "You saved his life," she said over and over. "You saved his life." But Ted was too busy being sick to say anything.

Ted stayed at home that day. When I walked past after school he was waiting for me, but he didn't scare me now. He stood in front of me and put his hand on my shoulder.

"Go away," I said.

"I got something for you," he muttered and he held his hand out. "It's a banana."

Elaine Canham

A Curse on Yesterday

Cara ran, splashing through the ruts made by the Romans' chariots.

"I hate the Romans," she muttered savagely, as the *thunk thunk thunk* of axes on wood got louder in her ears. Cara turned the corner and gasped. The oaks, the goddess Sul's sacred oaks, were falling. A branch, heavy with golden leaves, was tearing away with a splintering screech.

"No!" screamed Cara, and charged for the nearest axeman. She drew back her arm to strike him, but someone grabbed her from behind. She struggled and squirmed, but it was no use.

"Let me go! Let me go!"

"Cara! Cara, by all the gods, calm down!"

The red mists of her rage cleared a little and Cara saw Marbod, the fortune-teller.

"Marbod!" she said. "They're cutting down Sul's grove!"

The fat man looked shifty.

"I'm Marbodius, now, actually," he corrected her. "It's more up-to-date. More – er – Roman."

"But the trees – "

"There, there, my dear. They're going to build

Sul a temple, instead. I'm sure she'll be very pleased."

Tears welled up in Cara's eyes, but she shook them away crossly. Marbod had cut his hair and shaved off his moustache, as well as changing his name.

"You've turned into a Roman." She spat the last word.

He sighed.

"Look," he said. "Romans are the future. They're going to build a town here. Why, I'll have more animals to sacrifice than I can cope with. I'll be rich."

"But they've taken Father," said Cara, nearly bursting with grief and anger. "Some Roman soldiers came. Father went away with them – and – and he hasn't come back!"

Marbod sighed again.

"Oh my poor child," he said. "I'm very, very sorry. If there's anything I can do – "

"Yes!" Cara spoke fiercely. "There is. Send a message to the goddess for me."

Sul's spring gushed hot water and swirling steam. It smelled of power and bad eggs.

"What shall I tell Sul?" asked Marbod.

Cara peered through the steam, but she could not see the underworld where Sul lived.

"Say: 'Sul, great goddess, curse the Romans. Make them die in plague and battle.'"

Marbod hesitated.

"The Romans are going to build me a big altar, hollowed out on top to catch the animals' blood," he said, wistfully.

"Just write it down!"

Cara could not understand the symbols Marbod scratched on the little sheet of metal.

"Give it to the goddess," she ordered.

But Marbod backed away.

"Oh no. It's your curse, Cara. You give it to her."

Cara glared at him, stepped forward, and the steam wrapped her in writhing greyness. All was still, here, except for the bubbling of the water. The smell caught Cara's throat. A form appeared for a second in the steam, then vanished again.

"Goddess!" said Cara, loudly, so Sul wouldn't hear she was afraid. "Great goddess, hear me!"

A voice rose from the water, soft at first, then louder and louder.

"*Cara! Cara!*"

A warm breath brushed her cheek, and Cara jumped.

"*Shall you truly ask for so much death?*" whispered the voice.

Cara's heart thumped. Of course she wanted the Romans dead.

But now, through the steam, closer, closer, she could hear ghostly screams of pain, and long, long wails of grief: grief that she understood so very well.

"*Death, Cara?*"

Cara was suddenly furious with the whole world. "No!" she shouted. "Life!" And she flung the curse away and fled through the golden grove back to the world of the Romans.

Across the road she saw a man – and her heart leapt.

"Father!"

She pelted over to him and he caught her up and swung her round. She laughed in relief.

"I thought the Romans had killed you!"

He smiled at her.

"No, no, my love, of course not. I am Chief of the Tribe. We were talking about the plans for the town."

Cara looked up at him. He was wise, and brave – but he had talked to the Romans. He was going to work with them.

"But will you still be Chief?" she asked, bewildered.

"Yes, yes. Many things will change, but I will still look after the Tribe."

Cara tried to feel glad she had thrown away the curse.

But behind her she could still hear the sound of the axes on Sul's golden trees.

Sally Prue

21

UBBLE IN TROUBLE

When Toby's teenage brother, Ralph, went to the park to play football with his friends, Toby tagged along. But Ralph wouldn't let Toby play.

"You're useless," Ralph said. "Go and do something else."

So Toby, who was nine years old and usually cheerful, stamped angrily away. Some distance from the older boys, he wandered along the grassy edge of a cluster of trees, with clumps of leafy bushes growing among them. And there, nestling in a patch of clover under one bush, he found a strange purple ball, a bit smaller than a football.

He kicked it ahead of him, breaking into a run, dribbling the ball around several bushes before shooting fiercely into an imaginary goal between two trees.

"I'm as good as any of Ralph's lot," he muttered.

Then he stopped, staring. The ball had come to rest in some taller grass, deeper among the trees. But somehow it had started moving again, as if by itself, further into the grass.

And by the time Toby had blinked several times and looked again, the ball had disappeared.

"I'm seeing things," he said to himself.

Nervously he moved forward, still staring at the spot where the ball had been. Then he stopped again. He could hear a sound like someone crying, nearby. But he couldn't see anyone.

"Who is that?" he called. "Where are you?"

"It's me," said a small voice. "I'm here."

Toby took another step – and froze, eyes wide.

He had spotted the ball, half-hidden in the tall grass. But it had sprouted two short purple legs, two arms and a small purple head.

"Don't be afraid," the ball said. "I need help."

"Wh... what are you?" Toby stammered.

"I'm from another planet," the ball said. "My name's Ubble. And ... I can't get back into my spaceship."

He sounded as if he might cry again, and Toby's fright melted away. "I'm Toby," he said. "Why can't you? Where's your ship?"

"Up in the air, beside that tree," Ubble said, pointing. "It's invisible, so humans can't see it. And I can't get to it."

He had come to look at Earth, Ubble explained. So he had stopped his spaceship in midair over the park, made it invisible, then jumped out.

"I'm bouncy, so I don't need steps or anything," Ubble said.

But then, he went on, he found that he'd left his Shifter behind – the gadget that would lift him back up to his ship, or bring the ship down.

"So I'm stuck," Ubble said. "Unless you can help me, Toby."

"How?" Toby asked.

"Watch," Ubble said.

He picked up a pebble and threw it into the air. With a clang, the pebble bounced away as if from something metal.

"See?" Ubble said. "My ship's just there, not too

high. And the door's open. And since you're good at kicking..."

"Oh ... um ... sorry I kicked you, Ubble," Toby muttered.

"It didn't hurt," Ubble said. "I want you to kick me. Up to my ship, and through the door."

It sounded impossible to Toby. But he wanted to help Ubble. So – after making sure that no one was around – he tried.

When Ubble became a smooth ball again, Toby picked him up, then booted him high in the air. But Ubble bounced off the unseen ship and fell back.

"Missed the door," Ubble said. "Try again."

So Toby tried again. Over and over he kicked Ubble upwards – always missing the doorway that he couldn't see.

"I'm never going to do it," he said.

"You will," Ubble pleaded.

"Not unless I suddenly get a lot taller, with really long arms," Toby muttered.

And then his face lit up.

"I've got an idea!" he cried. "Hang on!"

He raced off, towards home, to gather what he needed.

Some long, light bamboo sticks that held up garden plants. Some string. And a long-handled fish-net that he used for scooping tadpoles out of ponds.

With all that he dashed back to the park, and put the puzzled Ubble into the net.

"You just fit!" he laughed.

Quickly he began tying the bamboo canes together, end to end. Then he tied them to the fish-net's handle, making it look like the longest net in the world – and the wobbliest.

But Ubble was light, and Toby's knots were tight. So it held together – just – as Toby lifted it. When he stretched up, Ubble was just high enough.

"Brilliant!" Ubble cried. "Go left ... more ... There!"

His arms and legs and head popped out again
as he leapt out of the net – and seemed to be
standing on empty air.

Then he picked something up. And Toby
blinked, as a big egg-shaped spaceship suddenly
appeared, floating in midair. Ubble stood in its
doorway, holding a glowing device – the Shifter.

"Thanks ever so much, Toby," Ubble called. "I
have to go now – I'm late – but I'll come back to
see you soon ... Goodbye!"

The ship's door closed, and it vanished again.

"Bye, Ubble," Toby said. Then he turned away
– just as his brother came ambling through the
bushes.

"What've you been up to?" Ralph asked.

"Nothing," Toby said. "Just kicking a lost ball..."

Douglas Hill

"Why do we still have to stay inside?" Jorry asked. "What if there aren't any monsters?"

"There are," said his sister Corry. "Trillions."

Jorry scowled. "Then why aren't there any here?"

But that was a question no one could answer.

Jorry and Corry were nine-year-old twins, whose mother was one of a group of scientists sent from Earth to study a faraway planet. As far as anyone could tell from Earth, the planet had good air and water, and seemed peaceful.

But on the way to the planet, the scientists turned on their spaceship's long-range scanners — and saw the truth.

Terrifying, enormous creatures swarmed all over the planet. Monsters – covered in armoured shells, or spines and spikes, or glistening slime – with many huge legs, or no legs at all like giant snakes – with mighty fangs or pincer jaws, vicious claws or cruel horns.

The scientists quickly decided to fly around the planet, instead of landing, and study it from above.

But then something went wrong in the ship's control system. They had to land, so it could be shut down and fixed. Otherwise, the ship wouldn't get back to Earth.

When they reached the planet, they landed in a pleasant valley – sunlit and open, with blueish turf, purple bushes and spindly pink trees.

And, strangely, not a single monster in sight.

But they set up a power-wall around the ship, in case any monsters appeared. Then they waited, inside the ship, while robots fixed the control system.

And no one complained – except the twins.

"It's silly, staying in!" Jorry told their mother that evening. "I don't think there are any monsters! We haven't seen any!"

"They could be anywhere," their mother said. "We can't take the risk."

"Even if we stayed by the ship?" Corry pleaded.

Their mother shook her head. "No one is going out. Certainly not you two."

But later, still grumbling in their room, the twins had an idea.

"If we could turn off the power-wall," Jorry muttered, "we could sneak out!"

"I think," Corry said, "I know how to turn it off."

"Really?" Jorry leapt up. "Let's go!"

No one was about as they crept along the passageway, towards a keyboard beside the airlock door. On its tiny screen, red letters said POWER-WALL ON. Corry tapped some keys. The letters vanished, and the airlock opened.

Nervously, excitedly, the twins stepped out.

In the pale light of two moons, they gazed around – at the thick turf, a bush with triangular leaves, a tree's feathery branches where a breeze sighed.

"It's lovely," Corry whispered.

"And spooky!" Jorry said.

As if in reply, the breeze's sigh became an eerie whine that made them shiver.

"We'd better go back in," Corry said.

"Let's take something!" Jorry said.

He snatched up a handful of turf, while Corry pulled a leafy twig from a bush. Then they hurried back into the ship, reset the power-wall and fled to their room, collapsing into giggles.

"Not a monster anywhere!" Jorry laughed.

Corry was peering at her twig. "Look! A bug!"

It was like a tiny yellow beetle with many legs, hiding under a leaf. Jorry poked at his bit of turf, and found more insects – two thread-like worms, and some red specks too small to see clearly.

"Where's the magnifier?" Jorry asked.

It was like a mini-camera, which Corry plugged into their computer and aimed at the insects. Then they looked at the screen – and nearly shrieked.

The insects, magnified many times, looked like enormous beasts – hard-shelled or spiky, with fangs or pincer jaws, many legs or none...

And the twins had seen such creatures before.

"Those are some of the monsters!" Corry gasped.

"But the scanners said they were huge!" Jorry said.

"It must have been when the control system went wonky," Corry said. "That must have made the scanners go wrong, too, so they magnified the bugs."

Jorry whooped. "Won't mum and everyone feel silly when we tell them..."

Then he stopped, and they stared at each other.

"We can't tell them," Corry said sadly. "We'd be in so much trouble, for sneaking out..."

And that was when their mother came in.

"Guess what?" she said excitedly. "The robots fixing the controls found that the scanners went wrong as well! Those monsters that they showed were just insects! Isn't that amazing?"

"Amazing," Corry said, looking innocent.

"I told you there weren't any monsters!" Jorry said. "So – when can we go out?"

Douglas Hill

32

Food for Thought

When Sam opened the front door and saw the monster there, he knew it was going to be a really rotten day.

Sam knew a monster when he saw it, and the thing on his doorstep was definitely a monster. It was three metres tall, it had scaly green skin with warts all over it, two tiny horns on either side of an enormous, ugly head, and what a smell!

"Right," it said. "I've come to eat you."

Somehow, Sam knew it was going to say that.

"It's nothing personal, mind you," the monster continued. "Head Office sent me, and here I am. My I.D."

The monster held out a card in its massive clawed hand. Sam looked closely at it.

"Human Eaters Co. Ltd," it said. The little colour photo matched the monster who was smiling at him.

"Oh," said Sam. "I suppose you'd better come in, then." Sam always tried to be polite, even when it was difficult.

"Nice place you've got here," the monster said as it followed Sam into the living room. "I like the carpet. I'll try not to leave any stains on it."

"Oh … thanks," said Sam. "Er … do you really have to eat me?"

"I'm afraid so," said the monster. "Orders are orders, after all. So, let's get it over with, shall we?"

"Isn't there anything I can do about it?" Sam asked.

"Not really," said the monster sympathetically. "We do have to go through the Riddle Game, though."

"The Riddle Game?" asked Sam. He'd always been good at riddles.

"Yes," said the monster. "It's part of the deal. We swap riddles until either you or I fail to answer one. If you fail, I go ahead and eat you. If I fail, I go away and you don't get eaten. But I won't fail. I never do."

The monster leaned back in the armchair, which creaked alarmingly. "Hey, that's a nice coffee table," it exclaimed. It reached over, picked the table up, and swallowed it. "Excuse me," it said. I haven't had anything to eat for ages."

Sam's stomach felt as if a dozen butterflies were wrestling inside it, because when the monster opened its mouth, Sam saw the teeth. They were long, sharp and well used.

"OK," the monster said, wiping a few splinters from its rubbery green lips. "No sense wasting time. I'll go first. What occurs once in a minute, twice in a moment, but never in a thousand years?"

Sam laughed. "That's pathetic. The letter 'm', of course."

The monster ripped off a chunk of the armrest and stuffed it in his mouth. "Look, I'm just getting warmed up."

Sam thought quickly. "What game do you play with wombats?" he asked.

The monster looked stunned. It stopped chewing and repeated, "What game do you play with wombats? What sort of a riddle is that? You could play anything with them! Golf, snooker, lawn bowls …"

"Is that your answer?" asked Sam.

"No! Let me think." It sat there, mumbling and muttering. Sam watched, and began to get excited. Perhaps he didn't have to get eaten after all.

The monster sat up suddenly. "I've got it! WOM! That's what you play with wombats!"

Sam slumped in his chair. "I thought I had you with that one."

"Nearly," the monster said. "You're not bad at this game. It's a pity I'll have to eat you when you lose."

"Thanks," said Sam.

"OK, what did the little dog say when it sat on the sandpaper?"

Sam looked at the monster, and he knew that his time had come. He put his head in his hands. Think! Dog on sandpaper … What do dogs say? What does sandpaper say?

"Time's up!" announced the monster. "Answer, please. What did the little dog say when it sat on the sandpaper?"

Sam could think of only one thing, so he said it hopefully. "Woof?"

The monster shook its head in sympathy. "So close … I thought you had it."

"So what's the answer?"

"Ruff. Rough, get it?" The monster roared with laughter.

"That's an awful riddle," said Sam, disgusted. "It sounds like one of those stupid ones you get inside Christmas crackers."

"So it should. That's where I got it from. Now, time to eat you." The monster paused. "No hard feelings? It's nothing personal …"

"No, no. You're just doing your job. Go ahead," said Sam.

"Wait." The monster pulled out a sheet of paper. "I have to do it properly." He unfolded the paper and began to read aloud. "I, as official representative of Human Eaters Co. Ltd, have won the Riddle Game, and am therefore entitled to eat the human named Sam Greeble, of 47 Hanover Street, Ringbark."

"Hold on!" interrupted Sam. "Did you say Sam Greeble?"

The monster frowned and looked at his paper. "Yes …"

"Of 47 Hanover Street?"

"Yes."

"That's next door. This is 45 Hanover Street."

The monster's jaw dropped. "I'm dreadfully sorry. How can I apologise enough for wasting your time?"

"That's OK," said Sam. "It could happen to anyone."

"I'll see myself out," the monster said. It rose, and ducked through the doorway. Sam heard the front door close, and smiled.

He never had liked Sam Greeble, anyway.

Michael Pryor

The Boy Who Made Things Up

There was once a father who had a little boy.
However, it was a bit of a waste for this father to
have a boy, really, because he was much too
interested in work. He worked all the week and
then, at the weekends, he spent all his time under
the car fixing it so that he would be able to go to
work again the next week. You will understand he
did not have much time to spend with his little
boy. In fact, all the little boy ever saw of his father
was a pair of boots sticking out from under the
car. This was not much fun. With no father to tell
him exciting stories, the boy had to make up his
own stories. He became very good at making
things up.

Well, one day the father's car broke down a
long way from home and had to be taken away
to a garage, and there was not much for the
father to do at the weekend. He felt bare and
unprotected with no car to crawl under. The
space of hills and sky made him feel nervous.
However, he decided to make the best of it all,
and take his boy for a walk instead.

"Come on, Michael," he called. "We'll wander
down to the cross-roads, shall we?" Michael was

delighted to go for a walk with his father. He marched cheerfully along beside him, looking at him curiously. He wasn't used to seeing all of his father at the same time. After a while he said, "Shall we just walk along, Dad, or shall we make some of it up?"

"Make some of it up?" said the puzzled father. "Make what up? ... Oh well, whatever *you* like, Michael," he added in a kind voice.

"Shall we go by *that* path then?" said the little boy, pointing. Over the field ran a path that the father did not recognize. It was narrow, and a bit tangled, with foxgloves leaning over it, and bright stones poking through the ground.

"That's funny!" said the father. "I've never seen that path before. There's no doubt you miss a lot by driving everywhere. Where does this path go?"

"It goes to the sea," said Michael, leading the way, brushing the dew off the foxgloves.

"But the sea is fifty kilometres away," cried the father. "It can't lead to the sea."

"We're making it up, remember," said Michael.

"Oh, just pretending," the father replied, as if everything was understood and ordinary again.

"The sea is on the other side of that little hill," Michael went on, and the father was amazed to see the path hump itself into a little hill in front of them. At the same time a soft murmuring filled the air as if giants were breathing quietly in their sleep. The father and Michael hurried up the little hill. There on the other side was the sea. The sand stretched a long way, starred with shells, striped with seaweed. There was no one else on all that long sunny shore. There weren't even any seagulls – just the sand, with the sea dancing along its edge.

"I told you. I told you," yelled Michael, and charged on to the beach. His father followed him, frowning with amazement.

"If I'd known we were coming here," he said, trying hard to make his voice sound ordinary, "I'd have brought buckets and spades."

"There are buckets and spades over by that log," Michael told him. "And our togs! Mine are wrapped up in a blue towel. What about yours?"

"Er..." said his father.

"Just make it up," Michael cried. "I'll make it up for you. An orange towel, almost new."

The log lay, half in, half out of the sand, as if it was trying to burrow down and get away from the sun. There were the buckets and spades. There were the togs and towels.

"Swim first!" declared Michael. "It's a bit coldish. Let's make it a warm day."

Immediately the wind died down and the sunshine grew hotter. The father stood frowning at his orange towel, almost new.

"I'm ready," Michael said, dancing before him. "You're slow, Dad. Last one in is nothing but a sand-flea." He sped, running and jumping, into the waves. The sand-flea father followed.

"Be careful!" he shouted. "Remember you can't swim, and I haven't done much swimming myself for a few years."

"Say you're a wonderful swimmer!" suggested Michael. "Say we can both swim to the islands."

"The islands?" said the father. Sure enough, out on the horizon were islands scattered like seeds in the furrows of the sea.

The boy and his father swam out to the islands without getting in the least bit tired. The water was warm, yet tingling, and as clear as green glass. Shoals of bright fish, as small and shiny as needles, followed them and tickled their feet.

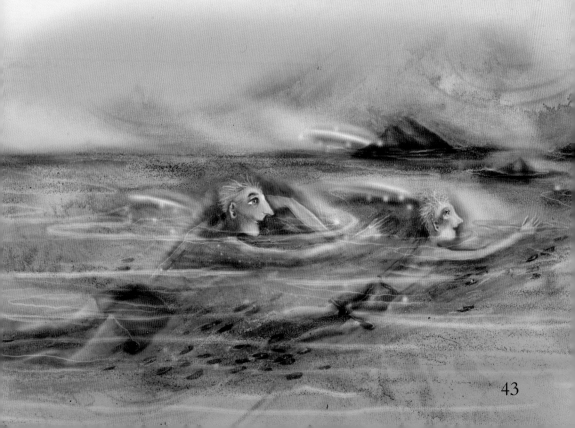

Down, down, far down under the water, the sand shone silver with black fish all over it, like a night sky pulled inside out. The boy and his father swam in and out among the islands. Waves burst on the rocks around them and rainbows in the spray curled over their heads. Sometimes they swam on their fronts, peering down through the clear water, watching fish and sand.

"I could swim all day," the father cried.

"But we've got to get back to our ice-creams," declared Michael.

So they swam lazily back to the long, empty beach, still quiet except for the sighing, breathing sea.

"Here! Where will we get any ice-creams?" asked the father, frowning again. "There are no shops."

"Can't you understand how things work yet?" Michael cried despairingly. "We make something up! Look!"

Far down the beach something was moving closer and closer. It was a tall thin man dressed in black and white squares, like a harlequin or a chess board. He was holding a blue frilly sunshade over his head with one hand and carrying a basket in the other. With his feet he furiously pedalled a yellow bicycle. As he passed them he put the basket into Michael's hands. Then he turned his bicycle and rode straight into the sea. For a few minutes his blue sunshade bobbed above the water and then a green wave curled slowly over it, like a curtain coming down at a theatre. They couldn't see him any more.

"See what I mean?" asked Michael. "Much better than a shop."

The basket was full of ice-cream with nuts in it, and strawberries on top. The father looked very grown-up and thoughtful. After they had eaten the ice-cream, they played with their buckets and spades for a while, and then they decided it was time to go back down the foxglove path. All the way home the father looked more and more thoughtful and grown-up. Every time he looked at Michael he blinked.

As soon as they got home, Michael was sent to wash his hands – a thing that usually happens to boys. The father stood beside the mother, drying up the dishes she was washing.

"Tell me, my dear," he said, in a quiet, nervous voice. "Does Michael often make things up?"

"Oh yes!" said his mother. "He's rather a lonely little boy and he's always making up some adventure. He's very good at it."

"But," said the father in a very astonished

voice, "he took me to the BEACH. We went SWIMMING. I got SUNBURNED. My shoes are full of SAND. And yet I *know* the sea is fifty kilometres away."

"Oh yes," said the mother very casually, "I told you. He's very good at making things up. I've told you before, but you were too busy listening to the car."

"It's very strange – very strange," said the father.

"But lots of fun!" the mother added.

"Yes, I suppose it is," said the father. He thought some more.

"I don't think I'll spend so much time with the car from now on. Michael needs the guidance of a father. A father and son should see a lot of each other, don't you think?" he asked.

"Oh yes, I'm sure they should," said the mother, and she smiled a smile that was almost a grin at the saucer she was washing.

Margaret Mahy

How to Win at Football

A new boy was coming to our school. We were excited when Mrs Khan told us that he was extra special. In assembly she said, "So we're all going to make him feel welcome, aren't we?"

When Danny turned up, he couldn't talk properly, couldn't write his name too well, and hadn't a clue about putting on his own trainers.

Danny was put into my class, right beside me. I'd much rather have had Wayne sitting near me because he's my best mate.

Danny needed a lot of help with everything so he had his own classroom assistant, Miss Driver. But Miss Driver only came in the mornings. When she wasn't there, Danny had to manage on his own.

Some people found Danny quite annoying, specially when he shouted out and wriggled on his chair when Mrs Khan was reading to us. Outside in the playground, he wrecked everybody's games. Wayne and I liked to play football with the rest of our gang. We went up past the bike-rack where we wouldn't bump into the little ones. But Danny kept rushing after us, grabbing our ball with both hands and running off with it.

Wayne said, "He's a pain in the neck, that new boy."

I said, "Yes, I know. My big cousin used to be like that."

My cousin Jason goes to college now. He still doesn't speak too clearly but I can usually understand him because he's very sensible and nearly grown up.

I said to Wayne, "I don't suppose Danny can help it," because that's what my grandad used to say about Jason.

Wayne said, "Course he can."

On the way home, I told my dad about the new boy always spoiling our fun. Dad said, "I dare say he's only trying to be friendly."

"Wayne says he does it on purpose to annoy us."

Dad said, "Or perhaps he's trying to say he wants to join in, even if he can't play? D'you remember how much your grandad used to enjoy the football, by cheering on his team?"

"Sort of," I said. I could just about remember Grandad sitting close up to the telly and waving a special wooden rattle.

When I told Wayne what my dad had said about the new boy, Wayne said, "Don't be daft! How could Danny join in? He doesn't understand the first thing about sport, let alone teamwork."

I said, "I'll find a way."

"Yeah yeah yeah," said Wayne. I knew he didn't believe me.

That night I stayed awake for hours trying to think how Danny could enjoy the football without being a pain to everybody else. Then I had an idea. I took Grandad's wooden football rattle to school. I told Danny, "This used to belong to my dad's dad. A long time ago, in the olden days, football supporters like my grandad used rattles like these to cheer on their team."

"Uhuh," said Danny, but I didn't know if he understood me.

I showed him anyway how to hold the wooden handle and how to twirl the rattle round and round so that it went clack-clacketty-clack.

Danny liked the sound it made. I told him, "My dad says we can borrow it." Then I explained to him that when we were playing football, instead of grabbing the ball, he must concentrate on making the clacketty noise.

Danny nodded.

"Uhuh, uhuh," he said. I think he understood.

On Friday afternoon, Wayne and my gang challenged some people from Class 6 to a Friday Friendly. We all went over to the far side of the playground. Danny was tagging along on my heels, same as usual. I gave him the wooden football supporters' rattle.

My gang began arguing. They didn't want Danny anywhere near the match.

"We know what he's like. We're bound to lose. He'll run off with the ball. Nobody'll have any fun at all."

I said, "Give him a chance. He's going to be our new cheer-leader."

Wayne didn't know what a cheer-leader was. "You'll see," I said.

I reminded Danny what he had to do. And he was brilliant. He ran up and down alongside the game shouting his head off and twirling the rattle above his head. There was so much noise of cheering and clack-clacketty-clacking that a crowd of kids came over to see what was going on.

This made my team feel important. We played even better than usual. Danny only tried to grab the ball once when he got over-excited but he handed it right back when I told him to.

We won 13-2.

"Not bad," I said.

"Not bad at all," said Wayne. The rest of them agreed.

When the bell went for the end of playtime, Danny lined up and walked into class and sat down in his place just like everybody else.

"Well done, Danny," said Mrs Khan. "You're really settling in, aren't you?"

Danny grinned but he didn't say anything.

Next week I'm going to show Danny another useful thing. I'm going to show him how to put on his own trainers instead of always taking mine.

Rachel Anderson

Doppelganger.com

You can find all kinds of cool stuff on the Web.
Yesterday I looked up a site that showed you how
to build a medieval catapult and one where you
hit cartoon penguins with a golf club and a site
with dancing hamsters and all the scripts for
Buffy the Vampire Slayer in Latin.

But then I got bored with just surfing. I'd have
had a go on my Playstation, but mum and dad
were watching some boring animal documentary
on the big TV downstairs. So I went looking for a
game to play or a puzzle or something really
weird.

And then I came across doppelganger.com. I don't even remember how I found it. The first page looked cool though.

Create your own doppelganger

it said.

Well, I thought I'd better do just that. Didn't seem to cost anything. Why not? So I entered the site.

The next screen had a questionnaire to fill in. A big one.

Name: William Mewes

Address: 127 Candlemaker Road, Edinburgh, ED2 2QE

Age: 12

Interests and hobbies: I didn't have any interests or hobbies that I could think of so I just put down 'surfing the net'.

Then I had to scan in a photograph of myself and I did that too. It was getting a bit boring now – not exactly a game or a challenge – I still wasn't sure what it was. But I'd come this far and I was curious to find out what doppelganger.com actually did. Eventually I completed the whole thing and pressed SEND.

A little yellow pop-up appeared.

> **Please wait while your information is being processed. This will take approximately 10 minutes.**

OK. Now I had nothing to do for ten minutes, and I couldn't use the computer. I sat and stared at the wall.

On the shelf opposite I suddenly noticed an Oxford Concise English Dictionary. Somebody must have given it to me as a present. I couldn't remember ever using it but suddenly I had an idea. I pulled it down, sat on the bed and looked up 'doppelganger'. If this was some sort of game after all, I wanted to be prepared. I thought that was pretty smart.

The entry said:

Doppelganger n. an apparition or double of a living person.

There was a ping from my PC and I glanced over at it.

I was on the computer screen. A picture of me. *I* was on the computer screen.

I got up from the bed and walked slowly across the room. The image on the PC was identical to me in every way, all except for the eyes. The eyes were empty and flat as paint.

Suddenly the boy on the screen turned his head and smiled at me. My heart lurched. Hardly breathing, I reached slowly for the mouse. Still smiling, his image followed the movement of my hand, then looked up at me and slowly shook its head. A caption scrolled across the bottom of the screen.

Your doppelganger will be with you shortly.

Internet zone

Then the screen went blank.

I tried to find the website again but it had disappeared. So I shut down the internet and turned off my PC.

I know it must be a trick. Only I don't know how they did it.

And they've got my address. I told the doppelganger where to find me.

I'm being stupid. It's a website. Things on the web can't hurt you.

It's not even real.

Is it?

Is it?

Is it?

Is it?

Jan-Andrew Henderson

The Rock: An Adventure in Oman

Zeinab's brothers went fishing every Friday.
Zeinab wanted to go with them. She followed
them to the beach and watched her brothers as
they prepared the boat.

"Go home, Zeinab. You're too young."

"Go home, Zeinab. It's too dangerous for you."

Disappointed, Zeinab turned around and made
her way back home.

That afternoon, Zeinab and her mother were
hanging out the washing on the flat roof of their
house when they heard a loud wailing and

shouting. They hurried down the staircase on the outside of the house and ran down to the beach.

A small boy had disappeared.

Most of the village was standing there, looking out to sea, hands shading their eyes from the glare of the sun. The boy's father and uncles dragged an old motor boat down to the water's edge. The boy's mother was up to her waist in water, and other women were pulling her back. A couple of pick-up trucks bounced along the sand in the other direction away from the beach, in case he had wandered off into the desert instead of the sea. But all of them knew.

Zeinab walked along the beach, and kept walking, scanning the empty sea for any sign of the boy. She kept walking and walking until the villagers on the beach were left far behind, and even the women's bright clothes had faded and become small black dots in the distance. The sun was getting low in the sky. It was time to turn round and head home, or the village would be looking for her too.

And then, as she looked towards a jagged outcrop of rocks, she saw a shape she didn't recognize. The shape didn't move, but it formed a new bump on the horizon. It was the boy – Zeinab knew it! The sea had spat him out onto a large rock, but had not given up on him. Wave after wave slapped against the rock, as if the sea wanted him back.

It was safer to go and get help. It was the sensible thing to do, but the waves were impatient and might not wait for her return. Zeinab kicked off her sandals and ran into the water. Her dress stuck to her body but she was used to the extra weight of her clothes in the water, and she struck out against the tide.

The waves crashed down on her head, and the salt water stung her eyes. I can't make it, she thought. I have to turn back before the waves take me.

But she kept on. Swimming strongly, she reached the rock and the frightened boy who clung to it. She called him, she pulled him, but the boy shook his head. The rock had saved him and he wasn't going to leave it.

Zeinab looked at the empty shoreline and at the waves creeping up over the rock, threatening to cover it all. She turned back to the boy.

"I won't let you drown," she promised him. "This is really easy for me," she lied. "My brothers and I swim to this rock all the time."

In the water, swimming next to the boy, she urged him on, half pushing and half carrying him. The beach seemed much further away this time, but it was there and she didn't move her eyes from it. And then suddenly the shallow water was beneath them and two sets of strong arms reached down to scoop them out of the foam.

The following Friday Zeinab went fishing with her brothers.

Julie Till

Zanzibar Treasures

For most of the year, tropical currents sweep the sweet smell of spices across the Zanzibar islands – but every July, they mysteriously change their course. Suddenly the tides change, washing strange treasures ashore. Last year, Kulsum's older brother Hamadi had found twenty rusty cans of brown shoe polish among the sand and seaweed. Unfortunately, no one Hamadi knew owned a shoe. So he travelled up to Stone Town on the early dala dala, to polish tourists' shoes. The money he made paid for a whole sack of maize flour. As June drew to a close, Kulsum and her little sister Samira started to imagine what this year's currents might bring.

"Maybe the jewellery box of a Persian princess," Samira thought.

"I heard of a boy who once found a case of Indian silk," sighed Kulsum. "Just think of the lovely dresses we could make for Eid!"

Finally it came, the first day of July. Samira and Kulsum could hardly sleep, they were so excited. They had to be at school at six-thirty to start sweeping the classrooms, so they decided to get up really early and head straight to the beach. As the muezzin called the village to prayer, they tiptoed carefully over their heavy-eyed parents and baby brother, and stepped out into the cool, still night. The two sisters ran barefoot past the mosque and into the woods.

"What if we really do find treasure?" Kulsum panted excitedly. "Do you think we could keep it?"

"No," said Samira. "But if we bought everyone in the village a present and then gave the rest to the Shehe, maybe he'd let us go to school in Stone Town."

The Shehe was the old village chief. He decided everything. Who married who, who got what when it came to the rice harvest – and so on. Usually, only the brightest boys got to go to secondary school in town.

"It would be nice if we could keep some of it," Kulsum complained. But she didn't hold out much hope. Everyone in the village shared everything. It was just the way things were.

The girls waited, eagerly looking out over the frothy waves. Their first discovery was a large white plastic bag, completely undamaged by the sea.

"Excellent!" cried Samira. "We can put the treasure in this."

For the next hour, all the girls found were plastic bags – torn ones. They soon had a dozen. Then suddenly Kulsum saw the belt of a rich sultan, studded with glistening rubies. She waded frantically out through the waves only to find that the jewels were nothing more than a red starfish, hitching a free ride on a worn-out piece of tyre.

"I suppose it might come in useful," sighed Samira, slipping the piece of tyre into the bag.

"Maybe we'll have better luck tomorrow," said Kulsum wearily, turning for home.

"What's that over there?" Samira exclaimed, pointing at something shiny in the distant sand.

They sprinted up the beach. Crashing onto their knees in the wet sand, the girls found an old coat – hanger. Disappointed, they dropped it into the bag and headed for home.

Dumping their booty in the house, the children quickly ate their maize porridge and mango and got ready for school.

"Habari za ashibui?" asked their mum as she combed their hair. "What's your news this morning? Are we going to be rich?" They shook their heads glumly.

After school the two girls went straight to the madrassa for their Koran studies before coming home for a late lunch.

"Shikamuu baba," they said, bowing respectfully to their father. Wearing the Islamic gown and hat he put on every afternoon after work, he was sitting cross-legged in the shade of a nearby orange tree. He was just putting the final elastic band around a large, tightly-scrunched plastic bag stuffed with torn bags.

"You made a football!" cheered Kulsum.

"I thought we might get all the children in the village together for a match tonight," he suggested. His daughters were thrilled.

"And what's that on your feet?" gasped Samira, pointing to his new sandals. She knew at once that the soles had been cut from the old piece of tyre they'd found, strapped to his feet by tightly wound palm leaves.

"I cut my foot on the rocks this morning looking for octopus," he told them. "But these sandals are just perfect. It won't happen again."

There was only one piece of treasure left out.

"What happened to the coat-hanger?" asked Kulsum, cautiously.

"Is that you, girls?" called their mum. "Dinner's ready."

The girls couldn't believe it. With a beaming smile, their little brother was waving a toy car, sculpted perfectly from the old wire.

"I think we should go treasure hunting tomorrow," suggested Samira as they washed their hands ready to eat their octopus and rice. "See what other riches we can find."

Adam Guillain